The Trump Effect : How one Leader is Reshaping America and the World

GORDON MILLS

Published by GORDON MILLS, 2024.

While every precaution has been taken in the preparation of this book, the publisher assumes no responsibility for errors or omissions, or for damages resulting from the use of the information contained herein.

THE TRUMP EFFECT : HOW ONE LEADER IS RESHAPING AMERICA AND THE WORLD

First edition. November 11, 2024.

Copyright © 2024 GORDON MILLS.

ISBN: 979-8227344731

Written by GORDON MILLS.

Table of Contents

The Trump Effect : How one Leader is Reshaping America and the World 1
Introduction | Defining "The Trump Effect" 4
Chapter 1 | Leadership by Disruption 12
Chapter 2 | Economic Boom and National Industry 16
Chapter 3 | Immigration and Border Control 24
Chapter 4 | The Middle East and Peace Diplomacy 31
Chapter 5 | Relations with Global Powers 36
Chapter 6 | Technology and the Future of Politics 44
Chapter 7 | Social and Cultural Shifts in the U.S. 55
Conclusion: The Legacy 66

THE TRUMP Effect

How One Leader is Reshaping America and the World

GORDON MILLS

THE
TRUMP EFFECT
How One Leader is Reshaping America and the World

GORDON MILLS

Introduction
Defining "The Trump Effect"

"To understand Donald Trump, you have to see him not just as a president or businessman, but as a force of nature—someone who disrupts and redefines the playing field entirely. Trump doesn't just look at political office as a means of government service; he views it as a platform for achieving massive transformation. He's the kind of leader who operates at the intersection of bold vision and relentless pragmatism. And that's where his genius lies. He doesn't care about the rules laid out by the Washington elite, nor does he worry about political niceties. His power comes from a deep understanding of what the American people feel, what they crave, and what they fear.

Take his approach to the economy, for instance. Trump sees American prosperity not as a given, but as something fiercely fought for. He's dismantling the regulations that have strangled American businesses for decades. He's incentivizing production right here on American soil, bringing manufacturing jobs back and prioritizing economic sovereignty. These are not just empty promises. Under Trump, you've got companies bringing billions of dollars in investments back home. The American people are not just being promised a better economy—they're seeing it happen in real-time, in tangible, measurable ways.

And he doesn't stop there. Trump is rewriting the narrative on foreign policy, too. Where past presidents sought diplomacy through appeasement and concessions, Trump asserts American strength. Look at how the world is responding. Suddenly, you have Russia expressing a willingness to cooperate, China talking about peaceful coexistence, and the EU turning to the U.S. for energy. This isn't accidental; it's Trump's design. He understands power dynamics on an instinctive level. He's shifting the global order by making it clear that America is not just a participant on the world stage—it's the lead actor. In short, Trump is orchestrating a reinvention of American power, and he's doing it in ways that shake the status quo to its core."

Trump's no ordinary politician. He's not in this game to make friends in Washington or cozy up to the establishment. He's here to fight for the average American, the ones who've been left behind by a system rigged for the elite. You've got career politicians who have spent decades doing nothing but making speeches and promising change. And then you have Trump—a man of action. A man who's about results, not rhetoric.

When he says he's bringing jobs back to America, he means it. He's not just cutting red tape; he's slashing it. Companies are moving their operations back, factories are reopening, and wages are rising. For the first time in decades, the American worker is a priority. This is economic patriotism, plain and simple. Trump understands that America can't be strong if its people are struggling. And that's why he's laser-focused on putting American interests first.

Look at the stock market. Look at Bitcoin. Both are hitting record highs. This isn't some Wall Street anomaly—it's the direct result of Trump's pro-business policies and his clear message to the world that America is open for business. And let's talk about national security for a second. Under Trump, there's no more coddling. No more bending over backwards to make other countries feel good while our own citizens suffer. The migrant caravans are breaking up, our borders are being enforced, and New York is finally taking steps to stop incentivizing illegal immigration. Trump's making it clear: if you want to come to America, do it the right way.

Globally, we're seeing a shift, too. Qatar is evicting Hamas leaders, China is calling for peaceful coexistence, and Russia wants dialogue. These aren't coincidences. Trump's strength is reshaping the world stage, and whether they like him or hate him, they respect him. And let me tell you, that's something America hasn't had in a long, long time."

"Donald Trump is not simply a politician—he's a disruptor of the established international order. He's not following the diplomatic playbook that has guided U.S. foreign policy for the last seventy years. Instead, he is pursuing a foreign policy that is profoundly transactional, marked by a pragmatic, almost ruthless pursuit of American interests. This approach has forced global powers to recalibrate. Trump's America is no longer the predictable ally, the reliable trade partner, or the restrained superpower. Instead, it is a nation demanding reciprocity, demanding respect, and, above all, demanding a return on its investments.

Consider the recent shifts in the Middle East. Under Trump's pressure, we see Qatar distancing itself from Hamas—a development almost unthinkable a few years ago. Even the Taliban, while still a complex and deeply challenging entity, is signaling openness to 'a new chapter.' Such moves reflect a world adjusting to an America that no longer plays by the usual diplomatic rules. Trump's message to allies and adversaries alike is unmistakable: the United States will not subsidize global stability without a clear benefit to its own citizens.

Then there's the economic dimension. Trump's focus on repatriating jobs and reducing trade deficits is a clear break from the globalist orthodoxy that has dominated U.S. policy for decades. And yet, the immediate effects are striking. Companies are returning, investments are growing, and the American economy is gaining momentum. For other nations, this signals a change in America's role. The U.S. is not merely a stabilizing power; it is a competitor and a self-interested player in an increasingly multipolar world. Trump's approach may seem chaotic, even dangerous to some, but it's undeniable that it's producing tangible shifts in both global perception and reality."

"In a global order that's been largely stagnant, Trump is a seismic force. He's not here to reinforce the old frameworks; he's here to dismantle them and build something fundamentally different. His actions signal to the world that the United States is undergoing a paradigm shift—one in which America's focus is firmly on its own prosperity, security, and influence. This is not isolationism; it's transactionalism. And it's changing how every major power interacts with the U.S., often in ways that defy conventional diplomacy.

Russia, for example, is signaling openness to dialogue, but let's be clear: this is less about friendship and more about strategic recalibration. With Trump, there's no pretense. He's not interested in making moral judgments or spreading democracy abroad. His question is always: 'What's in it for America?' This pragmatic approach resonates with some and horrifies others, yet it compels nations to reassess their positions. For China, it means finding ways to coexist peacefully without losing face. For the EU, it means pivoting on energy policy to reduce reliance on Russia and court American suppliers. Trump's America has fundamentally shifted the calculus for leaders worldwide.

But what about the repercussions of this approach? Trump's America demands results, not endless diplomatic posturing. He wants concrete benefits, visible impact, and measurable gains. And in this recalibrated order, global powers are forced to make hard choices. Will they align with America's newfound strength, or will they chart an independent path? Trump is not just a president; he's a phenomenon redefining what it means to be a global superpower in the 21st century. And the world is watching, calculating its moves, and adjusting to a U.S. that is anything but predictable."

"THE TRUMP EFFECT IS about more than just policies or speeches—it's a recalibration of what leadership looks like on the American and global stage. Trump isn't a product of the political machine; he's an outsider who forced his way into a system that didn't want him, and that's the key to understanding his impact. Unlike most presidents, who see themselves as stewards of tradition, Trump views himself as a reformer, someone there to shake things up, challenge the status quo, and deliver results for Americans who've been ignored by Washington for decades.

His influence on the economy is a prime example. Trump didn't just inherit an economy; he overhauled it. Through tax cuts and deregulation, he sparked a surge in job growth and investment that we hadn't seen in years. But it's not just the policy outcomes; it's the tone he set. Trump made it clear that America's economic interests come first. The companies bringing their production back to the U.S., the record highs in the stock market—these aren't random successes. They're the fruits of a focused vision that prioritizes American prosperity. Trump's message is straightforward: America isn't in the business of sacrificing its interests for global goodwill.

But his impact isn't limited to economics. Look at immigration. Trump doesn't view borders as abstract lines but as crucial components of national identity and security. His stance isn't softened by political correctness; it's defined by a commitment to protecting Americans. By enforcing immigration laws, Trump is saying, 'We are a nation of laws, not loopholes.' For too long, the political elite treated immigration as an issue to pander to, but Trump has transformed it into a defining matter of sovereignty and security. His approach sends a clear signal to the world: if you want to come to America, you play by the rules."

"THE TRUMP EFFECT IS nothing short of revolutionary. We're not talking about another smooth-talking politician who makes promises on the campaign trail and then toes the line in Washington. Trump came into office as a disrupter, someone who takes on the establishment with no apologies. And that's exactly what he's done. He's a man who speaks his mind, stands by his words, and fights for the people who put him in office.

Look at his influence on public opinion. Trump has redefined what it means to be a leader by throwing out the political playbook. He doesn't care about the mainstream media's approval or whether he's popular among elites. He speaks directly to Americans—the working-class folks, the forgotten men and women—who've been dismissed by politicians for decades. When he says 'America First,' it's not a slogan; it's a rallying cry. It's a promise to the everyday people who are tired of seeing their country treated like a doormat on the world stage.

Trump's policies on immigration are just as bold. For the first time in years, we have a president who isn't afraid to enforce our borders. He's calling out sanctuary cities, pushing for a border wall, and stopping policies that encourage illegal immigration. This isn't about xenophobia, as his critics claim—it's about common sense. Trump knows that a country without borders isn't a country at all. He's putting an end to the free-for-all that's threatened American security for far too long. And it's this fearlessness, this willingness to stand up to anyone—even his own party—that defines the Trump Effect. He's not here to play by the rules; he's here to rewrite them."

"To grasp the Trump Effect, you have to view it as a distinct, disruptive force that doesn't fit neatly into any historical mold. Trump's presidency marks a break from the post-World War II consensus that defined American foreign policy. He isn't interested in upholding an international order; he's rethinking it. Trump's view is that the United States is no longer a benefactor for the world. Instead, he sees America as a player in a global game where interests, not ideals, come first.

His economic policy reinforces this notion. Trump's America isn't interested in globalism; it's focused on a kind of economic nationalism that aims to return jobs and industries to American soil. This doesn't just challenge the economic practices of past administrations; it challenges the foundations of global trade. Companies relocating their operations to the U.S., tax policies aimed at keeping capital at home—these are parts of a strategic realignment that repositions America as a self-reliant, independent power. Trump has made it clear: the U.S. will not bear the cost of global stability if it comes at the expense of American prosperity.

Then there's Trump's foreign policy approach, which is unprecedented in its transactional nature. He doesn't see alliances as sacred commitments; he sees them as deals, subject to renegotiation if they no longer serve American interests. This shift has sent shockwaves through NATO, the EU, and beyond. Countries that have long relied on American support now face a United States that demands reciprocity. Trump's approach to diplomacy—direct, at times abrasive—forces allies and adversaries alike to reassess their assumptions. The result? An America that is less predictable, less accommodating, and, for better or worse, more assertive on the global stage."

"The Trump Effect isn't just a change in administration; it's a realignment of global expectations. Trump operates under a new set of assumptions, where U.S. engagement abroad is conditional on tangible benefits to Americans. This transactional mindset is altering the global order in profound ways. He's not interested in leading the world by example or championing universal values. Instead, Trump sees each international relationship as a negotiation—one where America's needs come first, and concessions are demanded in exchange for American involvement.

His stance on trade exemplifies this approach. Trump's tariffs, renegotiations, and insistence on favorable terms aren't the workings of a typical leader—they're the strategies of a businessman who expects a return on every investment. He's effectively telling the world that the U.S. is no longer willing to carry the economic burdens of others. This is a significant departure from the multilateralism that defined previous decades. In Trump's view, international agreements are not sacrosanct; they're tools to be adjusted, or discarded, when they no longer serve American interests.

The impact of this shift is evident in foreign relations, too. Trump's America doesn't assume the role of global mediator; it acts as an independent power willing to cooperate selectively and on its own terms. From his dealings with NATO to his approach to China, Trump is sending a message that America will engage when, and only when, it benefits. This forces every major player—whether ally or adversary—to reconsider their stance. The Trump Effect, then, is a recalibration. It's a world where the U.S. asserts its interests unapologetically, expecting other nations to respect its priorities or face the consequences."

Chapter 1
Leadership by Disruption

"Trump's disruptive style of leadership came at a time when Americans were feeling a profound sense of disillusionment with the status quo. For years, government systems seemed stuck, unresponsive to the needs of ordinary citizens. Trump saw this frustration and understood it. He didn't just tap into it; he gave it a voice. When Trump addressed the crowds at his rallies, he wasn't just promising change; he was leading a revolution against the conventional. I remember a specific moment when he called out the sluggish bureaucracies, saying, 'We're going to drain the swamp.' It struck a chord with people because it reflected what they'd been feeling for years.

Take, for example, his use of Twitter. He didn't just tweet for the sake of publicity; he used it to bypass traditional media, allowing him to connect directly with millions. Some may argue that these tactics were unconventional—even brash. But in reality, it was about reclaiming control over the narrative. I've seen firsthand how his unfiltered style resonates with Americans who feel they've been talked over by the political elite. Trump's approach didn't fit the typical mold, and that's precisely why it was effective. His supporters felt heard in a way they hadn't before, and his detractors couldn't ignore him. This is disruption in its purest form: shaking up a system to remind people of who really has the power.

It's also worth mentioning how this disruptive leadership went beyond rhetoric to real, tangible changes. His renegotiation of trade deals, particularly the USMCA replacing NAFTA, had a real impact on American workers. When I visited communities in Michigan, I heard stories from people who felt hopeful about manufacturing jobs coming back. His style didn't just change politics; it altered the lives of families who had felt left behind. Trump saw the value in breaking away from political tradition, and in doing so, he delivered results in a way that no one else dared to."

Trump's leadership was nothing short of revolutionary, and that's not just hyperbole. He took an approach that was long overdue, especially for people who felt ignored by the government. Trump wasn't afraid to stir the pot, to challenge the so-called 'rules' that Washington holds so dear. One example that sticks with me is his handling of NATO. Trump looked at the numbers and asked why America was footing such a massive bill when other countries weren't paying their fair share. His critics balked, saying he was endangering alliances. But Trump's point was simple: fairness. Why should American taxpayers carry the weight of defense spending if our allies aren't contributing equally?

This wasn't just about money; it was about standing up for the American people and saying, 'Your interests come first.' I'll never forget when he stood on that NATO stage, facing criticism from leaders across Europe. Instead of backing down, he doubled down, demanding that member nations pay their dues. That kind of boldness in leadership is rare, and it's precisely what makes Trump unique. He saw an imbalance and confronted it, no matter the diplomatic fallout.

Then there's the media. Trump didn't just criticize the press; he actively challenged its influence over public opinion. When he coined the term 'fake news,' it wasn't merely to insult reporters; it was a way of exposing media bias. And the people responded. From New York to California, I've met folks who tell me they're more skeptical now of news headlines, and they thank Trump for opening their eyes. I'm not saying all media is biased, but his confrontational style forced us to rethink what we accept as truth. That's leadership by disruption, and it's exactly what we needed to shake up the system.

Trump's disruptive leadership wasn't just a domestic spectacle; it had profound effects on America's global image. For better or worse, his unconventional methods made leaders worldwide sit up and take notice. I remember watching as Trump withdrew from the Paris Climate Agreement. Environmentalists were outraged, and the media was quick to condemn the move as reckless. But from Trump's perspective, it was about prioritizing American economic interests. He argued that the deal put the U.S. at a disadvantage by placing restrictions on American industries while allowing other countries, particularly China, to continue their emissions with little accountability. It was a controversial choice, no doubt, but it reflected his focus on American sovereignty over global consensus.

Trump's approach extended beyond climate policy. When he met with North Korean leader Kim Jong-un, the world held its breath. No sitting U.S. president had ever engaged directly with a North Korean leader, and experts were skeptical. But Trump's stance was clear: sometimes, disruption is necessary to break through decades of tension. I still recall the headlines calling it 'the handshake heard around the world,' a testament to Trump's belief in face-to-face diplomacy—even with adversaries. This is a leader who was willing to ignore diplomatic norms in favor of what he saw as practical engagement.

There is also the undeniable fact that Trump's approach inspired other leaders. Leaders in countries like Brazil and the Philippines found his defiance of global conventions refreshing and even empowering. They saw in Trump a model for challenging established systems, a way to exercise sovereignty without being beholden to multinational agendas. Whether we agree or disagree with Trump's methods, there's no denying that his style of disruption has redefined the boundaries of leadership in a globalized world.

TRUMP'S LEADERSHIP style has fundamentally reshaped the global landscape, and the ripple effects are far from over. His approach sent a message to the world that the U.S. would no longer follow international norms unquestioningly. For countries with populist movements or authoritarian-leaning governments, Trump's example was liberating. In Hungary, for example, leaders saw Trump's 'America First' rhetoric as validation for their own nationalist agendas. His willingness to withdraw from agreements like the Trans-Pacific Partnership and the Iran Nuclear Deal signaled that alliances and treaties are subject to American interests first. This was a powerful message, one that resonated globally.

But his leadership didn't just affect allies; it changed the game for adversaries too. Take China. Trump's trade war wasn't just an economic confrontation; it was a political statement. By imposing tariffs, he showed China that the days of passive trade policy were over. I spoke to several economists who pointed out that China had been testing U.S. limits on trade for years. Trump's actions—disruptive as they were—sent a clear signal that America would no longer tolerate economic practices it deemed unfair. His critics might argue this escalated tensions, but for those in Washington concerned about China's rise, it was a necessary correction.

Perhaps the most fascinating example of Trump's disruptive influence is his engagement with Russia. While past presidents maintained a strict distance, Trump's approach was different. He saw an opportunity for a relationship that could potentially keep adversarial forces in check. Though controversial, his strategy reflected a willingness to explore unconventional alliances. For Trump, disrupting the conventional wasn't just about shaking up domestic policy; it was about reshaping America's role on the global stage. The fact that leaders worldwide continue to discuss his policies, even with him out of office, speaks to the enduring impact of his leadership.

Chapter 2
Economic Boom and National Industry

When Trump came into office, he didn't just inherit an economy; he inherited a country with a wounded sense of economic pride. Americans felt the sting of lost jobs, shuttered factories, and a trade imbalance that tilted the scales against them. Trump's plan to revive American industry was straightforward but ambitious: bring jobs back to the U.S., cut taxes, and eliminate stifling regulations. It wasn't just rhetoric—it was a plan to rebuild America's backbone.

One of Trump's most significant contributions to the economy was his Tax Cuts and Jobs Act of 2017. This wasn't just a cut; it was a profound shift, lowering the corporate tax rate from 35% to 21%. This move was vital to making the U.S. competitive again, encouraging companies to reinvest here rather than abroad. It paid off. Shortly after the cuts, we saw companies like Apple and Amazon announce massive reinvestments. Ford brought manufacturing back to Michigan, GM expanded in Ohio, and we saw a new energy in American manufacturing.

Another crucial pillar of Trump's economic strategy was deregulation. For years, businesses had been suffocating under layers of federal regulations. I watched as companies, once bogged down by bureaucratic red tape, found new momentum under Trump's administration. A CEO I spoke with described it as taking the 'boot off our throats.' In 2019 alone, we saw GDP growth soar to 2.9%, a number that was unthinkable in the years before Trump. His vision for economic nationalism wasn't just about pride; it was about unleashing American potential.

Trump didn't just talk about economic nationalism—he implemented it in ways that sent shockwaves through global markets. His 'America First' policy was aimed at reducing America's dependence on foreign nations, especially China, for essential goods. I was there when Trump looked at the data on pharmaceuticals, electronics, and rare earth minerals, and he said, 'Why should we be dependent on countries that don't have our best interests at heart?'

Take the executive orders he signed to encourage the production of critical medical supplies domestically. During the COVID-19 pandemic, it became clear just how vulnerable our supply chains were. Trump recognized that and swiftly moved to incentivize U.S. companies to manufacture essentials right here at home. That decision wasn't just economic; it was strategic, giving America a more resilient economy.

The return of manufacturing didn't happen overnight, but we saw it begin under Trump's leadership. Companies like Intel committed to building semiconductor plants in Arizona, and Samsung followed suit. By putting tariffs on Chinese goods, he made it more attractive for American companies to produce here. I've spoken to business leaders who've told me that while tariffs were costly, the benefits of bringing production back to the U.S. outweighed the short-term expenses. Trump's push for economic independence was not a fleeting agenda; it was a long-term shift designed to make America stronger and self-sufficient in ways we haven't seen in decades.

The Trump administration brought with it a unique energy in global markets. Investors saw in Trump a leader who was unafraid to push for economic growth aggressively, even if that meant taking risks. His presidency was marked by confidence in market-driven success, and that confidence was contagious. During Trump's tenure, the stock market reached record highs. In 2019, for instance, the Dow Jones soared past 28,000—a psychological milestone that reflected optimism in Trump's tax and regulatory policies. Investors were willing to put capital into U.S. markets because they believed in the administration's commitment to business and growth.

Trump's impact on cryptocurrency was equally fascinating. Although he was publicly skeptical of Bitcoin, the broader investment environment under Trump was one that welcomed risk-taking and innovation. The years of his administration were some of the most active for cryptocurrency, as low interest rates and a growing acceptance of alternative investments led Bitcoin to unprecedented heights. By 2020, Bitcoin hit $30,000, and analysts attributed much of this surge to the high-risk appetite fostered in part by Trump's policies.

Another critical area of Trump's economic influence was his ability to turn American markets into a safe haven amid global uncertainty. During trade tensions with China, U.S. markets became even more attractive to international investors seeking stability. By pushing for self-reliance, Trump made the U.S. an economic fortress of sorts, creating a climate where foreign capital flowed into American assets. This wasn't accidental; it was part of Trump's larger vision to strengthen America's financial standing globally.

Trump's economic policies have ignited a trend of nationalism that's now influencing countries beyond America. What he demonstrated was that a nation could prioritize its own industries without entirely abandoning globalization. The 'America First' approach was more than just economic policy; it was a blueprint that resonated with leaders worldwide, from Europe to Asia. Leaders saw Trump's determination to bring back industries and thought, 'Why aren't we doing this?'

A real example of Trump's influence on national industries can be seen in the automotive sector. His tariffs on imported steel and aluminum, as well as his renegotiation of NAFTA into the USMCA, directly encouraged companies to expand their U.S. operations. One automotive executive told me that Trump's tariffs created a 'tipping point' that convinced them to open a new factory in the Midwest. The jobs created by these policies were more than numbers; they were a revival of middle-class pride in places that had seen economic decay for years.

Globally, countries are now more cautious about overreliance on international supply chains, a trend accelerated by the pandemic. Japan, for instance, has implemented policies to reduce dependency on Chinese manufacturing—a move reminiscent of Trump's strategy. This shift towards economic nationalism and supply chain security isn't just a trend; it's a paradigm shift that will define international economics in the coming years. Trump's influence, therefore, extends beyond the borders of the United States. The precedent he set is now part of a global dialogue on self-reliance, industrial sovereignty, and economic resilience.

Trump's economic strategies sparked a resurgence in American industry, providing a blueprint for economic nationalism. These policies, though controversial, showed the world that prioritizing national industry could be not only beneficial but transformative. The return of jobs to U.S. soil, the record highs in the stock market, and the growing independence in critical supply chains are testaments to a disruptive approach that changed the economic landscape.

Under Trump, American workers in industries that had long been in decline saw new hope. Towns across the Rust Belt witnessed factories reopening, offering jobs to communities that had once faced economic despair. This was the tangible result of an agenda that valued national strength over global dependence. In this sense, Trump didn't just bring back jobs; he restored a sense of pride and purpose to millions who had felt overlooked by globalization.

For the world, Trump's policies offered a case study in economic self-sufficiency. Leaders in Europe and Asia observed Trump's tactics and began reconsidering their reliance on foreign production. Countries like India and Australia have started implementing policies to encourage domestic manufacturing, a nod to the broader impact of Trump's approach. His influence has, without question, redefined what's possible in national economic policy, setting a precedent that will influence global leaders for years to come.

The economic boom of the Trump era was not only about numbers and market gains; it was about reaffirming the belief that a nation's wealth should serve its own people first. In this way, Trump's legacy on the economy goes beyond mere policy—it's a movement that challenges conventional views on trade, labor, and economic sovereignty. This was an era defined by the belief that America could stand on its own, and the ripple effects of that belief are still shaping economies worldwide.

Reflecting on these economic shifts, the results are hard to ignore. For those of us who grew up in towns where the factory whistle once punctuated the rhythm of life, Trump's policies struck a chord. My hometown in the Rust Belt—like countless others—was once vibrant, powered by steel mills and assembly lines. But when the jobs disappeared, so did a lot of hope. Trump's "America First" agenda, whether you agreed with his methods or not, sparked something different. He took an economy used to outsourcing and brought it back to Main Street, making places like Ohio and Michigan part of the national story again.

Take, for instance, the shift in manufacturing jobs. I remember visiting a factory in the Midwest in 2018, where new hires—many who hadn't worked in years—were being trained. One man told me he felt as though he'd been "given a second shot" at life. The ripple effect in these communities was palpable. When factories are running, the restaurants fill up, the small shops stay open, and families can thrive instead of just getting by. The return of manufacturing doesn't just add to GDP; it restores the sense of self-worth for American workers, especially those who once thought their trade was obsolete.

The steel and aluminum tariffs, though controversial, were a prime example of this change. In late 2018, I spoke with a steelworker in

Pennsylvania who had been laid off twice in his career due to outsourcing. He told me, "These tariffs might cost us more in some areas, but for once, it feels like the government is standing up for us." Sure, critics pointed out the impact on prices, but for people in industries long abandoned, the policy symbolized a re-commitment to the American workforce.

On Wall Street, Trump's policies didn't just influence investors but actually reshaped how they approached the American market. The 2017 corporate tax cuts were a game-changer. We saw immediate responses from major corporations. Apple's announcement to invest $350 billion in the U.S. economy was a testament to the renewed confidence in America's business climate. The job creation and infrastructure improvements from these reinvestments provided tangible benefits, yet this wasn't just about adding jobs or capital; it was about companies taking pride in being American again.

This pride also permeated the high-tech industries and emerging markets. Under Trump's administration, we witnessed an unprecedented rise in technology investments. From Elon Musk's Gigafactories to Amazon's expanded warehouses, tech giants found the U.S. to be a prime site for growth. Even Tesla, which seemed perennially on the brink, saw meteoric growth, not only in the value of its shares but in its global influence. What's fascinating is how much of this could be traced back to Trump's broad brushstrokes of economic nationalism and tax incentives that lowered the barriers for tech innovation in America.

I recall a conversation with an economist friend who observed that "economic nationalism," often seen as a throwback to the past, was actually helping to future-proof the U.S. economy. At a time when global supply chains were fraying, Trump's moves to bolster domestic production offered a kind of insurance policy for the U.S. And when COVID-19 hit, this approach proved prescient. We saw firsthand the consequences of depending on foreign production for critical goods. Trump's emphasis on "Made in the USA" meant that, while still challenging, the country was better prepared to meet the needs of its people during the crisis.

And then there's cryptocurrency—a story no one expected to be part of the Trump era's economic legacy. Despite Trump's own skepticism of Bitcoin, his policies fostered an environment that encouraged investment in alternative assets. Between 2017 and 2020, Bitcoin skyrocketed from roughly $1,000 to nearly $30,000. Part of this can be attributed to the broader economic conditions created by Trump's administration, which made people more open to exploring new investment avenues. In fact, there were stories of small-town investors who took advantage of this boom to significantly improve their own financial stability. The bull market in cryptocurrency wasn't solely due to Trump, but the high-risk, high-reward spirit he encouraged in the economy certainly played a role.

Moving forward, one of the lingering effects of Trump's presidency is the awareness it raised about economic vulnerability. By bringing attention to issues like supply chain resilience and job repatriation, he didn't just impact the present; he changed the narrative for the future. Today, leaders across the political spectrum, even those critical of Trump, are emphasizing the need to bring essential industries back to U.S. soil. This shift toward economic sovereignty has staying power, and we can trace much of it back to the policies set in motion during those four years.

On the global stage, Trump's influence is evident in more than just American businesses. Countries like Japan, Australia, and parts of Europe have embraced similar measures to promote domestic production. Recently, I had a conversation with an Australian economist who noted that, while his country didn't always agree with Trump, they couldn't ignore the value of some of his economic strategies. "He forced us to rethink our dependencies," he said. Australia is now encouraging businesses to reduce reliance on China for critical goods—a direct nod to Trump's playbook on economic self-reliance.

In many ways, Trump's economic policies were a double-edged sword, wielding a mix of benefits and challenges. But for those who found new jobs, who saw their hometowns recover, or who watched American businesses grow stronger, the impact was undeniable. These policies reminded us that, sometimes, rebuilding at home requires bold moves, even if they shake up the status quo. And in an era defined by global interconnectedness, Trump's presidency proved that a bit of economic nationalism could, in fact, be a powerful tool for creating local resilience and global stability.

Chapter 3
Immigration and Border Control

In the complex landscape of U.S. immigration policy, Trump's stance has consistently championed stricter border control and a rethinking of benefits for undocumented immigrants. These efforts align with his fundamental philosophy: America first, with a clear-cut distinction between legal and illegal immigration. Unlike past administrations that tried to find middle ground, Trump's policies on immigration—whether we're talking about the southern border or sanctuary cities—left little room for compromise. The recent policy moves, such as New York City's decision to discontinue benefits for undocumented immigrants, are emblematic of a shift that reflects his influence even outside his presidency.

For instance, take the decision by NYC—a sanctuary city long recognized for its leniency toward immigrants—to halt its distribution of benefits like debit cards to undocumented individuals. This is a landmark moment, essentially highlighting a city that has long opposed Trump's immigration policies now adopting measures that are more in line with his vision. This shows that Trump's influence on immigration goes beyond legislation; it's about how Americans, and now even leaders in liberal strongholds, are beginning to view the resources allocated to citizens versus those provided to non-citizens. This shift marks a recalibration of values—one where the city is effectively reassessing its priorities and perhaps coming to terms with the need to address its own citizens first in times of economic and social strain.

What's critical here is the broader message: this isn't just about providing or denying benefits; it's a statement on the costs and impacts of unregulated migration. Historically, cities like New York have been safe havens, seeing themselves as guardians of immigrant rights and inclusivity. But Trump's administration challenged that narrative by consistently emphasizing the pressure undocumented immigration puts on local resources. We see this now in the subtle but powerful decisions even sanctuary cities are making as they shift their policies. Trump's relentless drive to enforce a rigid immigration policy encouraged cities to reconsider the ramifications of open-door policies. In this context, NYC's move is not just a local decision but a significant endorsement of the logic Trump has long advocated: prioritizing citizen welfare and resources as a fundamental responsibility of governance.

Migrant caravans breaking up before reaching U.S. borders is another testament to the enduring impact of Trump's stance on immigration. These large-scale caravans, primarily from Central America, were once common sights, representing collective efforts of thousands seeking refuge and a better life. The consistent pressure applied during Trump's presidency led to international collaborations, such as agreements with Mexico and Guatemala, to control and intercept these groups before they reached the U.S. southern border. These caravans didn't disappear by happenstance; they were disrupted by an administration unafraid to address immigration with a stark "zero tolerance" attitude.

The broader implications here cannot be understated. By pressuring neighboring countries to take a more active role in managing these mass migrations, Trump sent a clear signal: America could no longer be the default endpoint for everyone seeking a new life. This ripple effect has pushed Latin American countries to confront their own immigration issues, often at the request of the U.S., creating a regional accountability model. Leaders in Mexico, who previously criticized Trump's immigration policies, have found themselves working within the framework he established, reinforcing borders and enhancing their own internal enforcement mechanisms. This cooperation underscores a shift in immigration policy, where the responsibility is shared across borders rather than resting solely on the United States.

When analyzing the breaking up of these caravans, the economic aspect also comes to light. Trump's threats to impose tariffs on Mexican goods if the country failed to help manage the migrant flow was a clear example of his unique approach to foreign policy—using economic leverage to drive security goals. This economic strategy was effective, compelling Mexico to increase security at its southern border and deploy its National Guard to curb migrant movement. Here, Trump's approach to immigration reform becomes apparent as not just about border walls and enforcement but as a comprehensive negotiation of economic interests and diplomatic relationships.

But Trump's policies on immigration go beyond controlling the flow of migrants. His administration's emphasis on the moral dimensions of border control highlighted a return to the concept of national sovereignty. By focusing on the legal versus illegal debate, Trump essentially reframed the national discourse on who has the right to be in America. For decades, U.S. immigration policy had become increasingly flexible, welcoming a mix of legal and undocumented immigrants. Trump's policy decisions, however, reminded Americans of the importance of regulated immigration. By actively enforcing policies that restricted unauthorized entry, he made border security a critical pillar of national identity.

What's also striking is the tone and messaging behind these policies, and this is where Trump's influence becomes unique. While other administrations addressed immigration in cautious, often bureaucratic terms, Trump's approach was direct, unapologetic, and, to some, aggressive. Yet, it resonated with a large segment of Americans who felt that previous leaders had neglected the impact of unchecked immigration. The emphasis was on national security, job protection, and the idea that no one has the inherent right to cross U.S. borders without permission. It's a philosophy that, though divisive, injected a new kind of vigilance into the American consciousness regarding immigration.

Critics argue that this strict approach lacks compassion, while supporters counter that it's an overdue assertion of America's right to self-determination. Both perspectives have validity, but there's no denying that Trump's policies have pushed other world leaders to reassess their immigration frameworks. We see European countries implementing policies to control migration flows and toughen asylum rules—trends that have echoed Trump's own approach. Even Canada, traditionally known for its open-door policy, has seen its leaders adjust to new immigration norms, reinforcing stricter screening and turning away irregular migrants at higher rates.

Trump's policies on immigration reform also contributed to a renewed sense of control over the American job market. One of the key arguments has been that an oversupply of low-skilled labor leads to wage stagnation for native workers. By prioritizing American workers and tightening the border, Trump sought to create an environment where citizens and legal residents could compete for higher wages without the pressure of an influx of low-wage, undocumented labor. Supporters of Trump argue that this focus on the American workforce has empowered working-class citizens who often felt they had been left behind in the era of globalism.

The shift in policies to halt benefits to undocumented immigrants is not just about the immediate financial implications. It's a fundamental question of who the government should prioritize. Proponents of this shift argue that it's a necessary reallocation of resources to citizens in need, while critics view it as a disregard for the humanitarian aspect of immigration. But the tangible impact is there: By halting these benefits, cities are effectively signaling a reorientation of their priorities. This policy shift indicates that even traditional liberal enclaves are reconsidering how they balance humanitarian goals with practical governance.

For those who criticize Trump's immigration policies, it's often his style that incites opposition. Yet it's that same style—unfiltered, unyielding—that has made his policies so effective and impactful. Trump forced Americans to confront difficult questions: How many resources can the U.S. afford to extend to undocumented immigrants? Where should the lines be drawn in terms of access to public services? Should American borders be as permeable as they have been in the past? These aren't simple questions, but Trump's policies prompted the nation to face them head-on.

In looking back at the evolution of U.S. immigration policy, Trump's era stands as a clear turning point. While many of his policies remain contentious, they reflect a clear ideological stance on sovereignty, national identity, and the responsibilities of citizenship. His approach was not without flaws or critics, but for those who believe in a firm and unwavering national border, Trump's actions represented a long-awaited recalibration of immigration norms.

One example that truly brings this shift to life is the story of a small town near the Texas-Mexico border. For years, they faced challenges that felt insurmountable: crime rates spiking, local resources stretched thin, and residents growing increasingly concerned about their safety. A few locals shared their perspectives on the new policies. Mary, a 67-year-old resident, explained that for years she'd been frustrated seeing her community lose its footing. She grew up watching her parents build up the town, brick by brick, only to watch the community strain under increased immigration that outpaced local resources. "I want everyone to succeed," she said, "but I want to feel safe and know our resources are going to those who built this town."

These personal stories are woven into a national narrative Trump has brought to the forefront: ensuring that communities and individuals don't feel overlooked. For Mary and others, Trump's immigration policies are about safety, about knowing that those within a community have everyone's best interests at heart. The idea here isn't opposition to newcomers but rather a request for order and security that resonates deeply with people who have seen their neighborhoods change in unexpected ways.

The tangible impact of tightened immigration policies, especially those targeting unauthorized entry, has been felt in many sectors beyond safety. For example, in the healthcare system, stricter regulations have reduced the strain on emergency rooms in high-traffic areas near the border, according to data published by regional health boards. These hospitals have seen a noticeable reduction in non-emergency visits, allowing doctors to focus resources on critical cases. This is the real-world effect of Trump's policies that resonates with many Americans: a healthcare system that feels a little less overwhelmed and resources that stretch just a little bit further.

During his tenure, Trump also emphasized the need to support American workers by limiting the availability of low-wage jobs to undocumented immigrants. This approach, though controversial, has proven to be a critical aspect of Trump's economic strategy. And while critics argue it limits opportunities for those seeking a better life, supporters see it as an effort to boost the earning potential of American citizens. John, a mechanic from Detroit, summed it up well: "I know what it's like to scrape by on low wages. I want to see jobs go to people who work hard, pay their dues, and are here legally."

His policies spoke directly to people like John, who felt that their livelihoods were sometimes overshadowed by a global workforce dynamic that left them competing for wages. By encouraging policies that discouraged illegal immigration, Trump not only shifted the economic playing field but created a climate where working-class Americans felt like they had someone advocating for them. And in an age where wage growth had stalled, these measures brought a new sense of hope to many. In 2019, the U.S. Bureau of Labor Statistics noted a 3.1% wage growth in industries with traditionally high undocumented labor, hinting at Trump's policies making an impact on wage competition.

What really stands out when reflecting on these policies is how Trump took immigration, which had often been viewed primarily through a humanitarian lens, and reframed it as a matter of national and economic security. This pivot wasn't just about border control—it was about making sure that U.S. policy accounted for the rights and needs of American citizens first. His approach might seem rigid, but it fundamentally changed the national conversation, making Americans, whether in urban cities or rural towns, feel their concerns were validated.

Analyzing Trump's impact on immigration brings us back to the question of long-term implications. Critics worry about the image these policies might project on the international stage, yet we see that other nations are also recalibrating their approach to immigration. It's clear that these policies don't only exist in an American vacuum; they are part of a global shift in how countries address the challenges of migration.

Chapter 4
The Middle East and Peace Diplomacy

Trump's approach in the Middle East has defied conventional diplomatic pathways, reshaping alliances and resetting dynamics that many deemed intractable. The region, historically dominated by complex relationships and perennial conflict, witnessed substantial shifts under Trump's policies, with ripple effects that persist. Key decisions—ranging from urging Qatar to expel Hamas leaders to brokering diplomatic relations between Israel and multiple Arab states—indicate a legacy of pushing for change, not through traditional diplomacy but through actions designed to create visible, immediate shifts.

At the core of Trump's Middle East approach is a brand of diplomacy rooted in directness and expectations for rapid, tangible results. Take Qatar's decision to evict Hamas leaders: this was a move signaling that regional players are willing to take a hard line against groups that disrupt stability. Previously, Qatar had faced criticism for hosting Hamas leaders, which, in the eyes of Trump's team, indirectly enabled Hamas's influence in Gaza and beyond. But Trump's persistent calls for accountability in the Middle East put pressure on Qatar to make a decision that symbolized a break with the past. Qatar's response was a clear indicator of Trump's influence, one that pushed the country to align more closely with Western interests in isolating extremist factions.

For years, political experts believed that an organization like Hamas, with its entrenched position in Palestinian politics, would never be amenable to genuine peace talks. But after seeing Trump's steadfast commitment to peace agreements with nations like the UAE and Bahrain, even Hamas showed signs of reconsideration. Trump's unorthodox methods seemed to drive home the message that peace and prosperity in the Middle East could only emerge through engagement rather than endless resistance. At a conference in 2020, a senior Hamas official noted, "The dynamics are changing, and we cannot ignore them." For many, this was a startling admission that Trump's methods might have opened the door, however slightly, for a reevaluation of strategies within the organization.

The Taliban's recent language about a "new chapter" is another outcome that could be linked to Trump's approach. By holding firm on his intentions to withdraw U.S. troops from Afghanistan—arguably a symbolic end to decades of U.S. military presence—Trump sent a strong signal to regional factions: the U.S. was no longer interested in protracted conflicts but was open to diplomatic channels. The Taliban, once notoriously resistant to any Western negotiation, started framing its public messaging to appeal more to international audiences, seeking legitimacy rather than isolation. The statement about a "new chapter" reflects a shift in perspective, a signal that the Taliban wants to be seen as more than just a militant group; they aspire to establish a role in Afghanistan's governance, perhaps even in a capacity that respects international norms.

In response to these statements, Trump's allies argued that these diplomatic shifts resulted from America's pivot away from prolonged conflicts and costly interventions. Trump himself echoed this sentiment in his speeches, often stressing that it was time for Middle Eastern nations to determine their own futures without undue dependence on the U.S. "We can't keep being the police force of the world," he asserted, emphasizing a strategic recalibration that meant military presence was no longer the default answer to international crises.

A broader analysis from global experts indicates that Trump's strategy went beyond immediate tactical gains. The push for self-reliance and stability within the Middle East represents a broader ideological shift in how the U.S. engages with the region. Leaders from Egypt, Saudi Arabia, and even Turkey have echoed support for this approach, with some openly recognizing that it is time for the region to pursue internal solutions and self-driven governance reforms. Turkey, which had often found itself at odds with U.S. policies, publicly acknowledged that a more autonomous Middle East would foster stronger, more balanced partnerships with Western nations.

Trump's influence on the Middle East not only reflects a reshaping of the diplomatic stage but brings a personal reminder of what it means to push boundaries in the pursuit of peace. The impact of his methods is felt deeply across a region historically mired in endless conflict cycles. When I think about Qatar's decision to evict Hamas leaders, it isn't just about a policy shift; it's about Qatar stepping forward to say, "We are serious about aligning with a broader vision of stability." By choosing to remove a group that has long fueled regional tensions, Qatar sends a clear message that they're embracing a new role in promoting peace and cooperation. It's like a neighbor finally agreeing to turn down the volume, showing respect for the whole neighborhood—everyone breathes a bit easier.

One story that stays with me is the Abraham Accords. To see countries like the UAE and Bahrain come forward, shake hands with Israel, and sign agreements that would have been unthinkable just a few years back—it's as though generations of animosity suddenly found an off-ramp. A businessman in Dubai, who used to view Israel as an untouchable competitor, now openly discusses trade ideas with Israeli counterparts. "I never imagined I'd be working with Israelis, let alone having coffee with them," he remarked in a recent interview. These moments reveal how Trump's brand of diplomacy created real-life bridges, allowing everyday people to experience the profound difference peace can make.

The Taliban, too, presented an unexpected turn. To hear them speak about a "new chapter" reflects a significant departure from their former stance. Though still a contentious issue, the mere suggestion of a Taliban willing to shift toward governance shows how Trump's influence may have sown seeds for a peace that could last. His "America First" stance meant stepping back from an automatic military response and inviting other groups, even longstanding adversaries, to consider diplomatic solutions. When the U.S. troop withdrawal was announced, I remember a U.S. veteran, now a civilian contractor, saying, "I finally feel like this cycle of deployment after deployment might end." These stories bring the impact into sharp focus—not just for officials in distant capitals but for families and soldiers who lived through these choices.

As I look back on the ripple effects, I see a Middle East that's stepping into a future of self-defined peace and stability, rather than one forced upon it. Statements from key leaders reinforce this shift. Crown Prince Mohammed bin Salman, for instance, has discussed his Vision 2030 with a renewed sense of optimism, envisioning Saudi Arabia as a major player in the international community. Even Egyptian President Abdel Fattah el-Sisi noted in a recent speech, "This is our moment to create an Arab world defined by innovation and prosperity, not endless war." It's clear that this realignment represents more than policy—it's a cultural evolution that promises long-term change.

And then there's the data, which serves as a powerful backdrop to these stories. According to the International Monetary Fund, regional economic forecasts have taken an optimistic turn following peace accords. Foreign investments are flowing into Israel from Gulf nations, and trade between former adversaries has begun to grow. Statements from economic analysts echo the sentiment that Trump's leadership style brought an energy that translated into tangible outcomes in the market.

It's a reminder that diplomacy doesn't just change headlines; it changes the bottom line.

I see these changes as profound steps forward for a world that has grown weary of traditional power dynamics. It's not just about politics anymore; it's about creating environments where peace can flourish, allowing innovation and progress to replace cycles of fear and tension. The Trump Effect, as I see it, is ultimately a reimagining of what's possible in the realm of international relations. By elevating national interests in a way that harmonizes with global stability, Trump has left an indelible mark—one that we may only fully appreciate with time.

Chapter 5
Relations with Global Powers

The diplomatic landscape surrounding U.S. relations with Russia, China, and the EU has undeniably shifted. Trump's unyielding approach to reestablishing American primacy—an approach that sometimes meant distancing allies and confronting adversaries with unexpected moves—has catalyzed renewed engagement from global powers that now seems intent on resetting their relationship with the United States. This isn't mere rhetoric. Each power's latest overtures show a willingness, albeit cautious, to find common ground. But beneath this surface interest in "peaceful coexistence" lurks a broader set of strategic calculations that we cannot ignore.

Take Russia, for instance. Trump's stance towards Russia has been a sharp departure from previous administrations. Instead of treating Moscow as a default adversary, Trump adopted a tone that mixes deterrence with occasional collaboration. Putin's recent willingness to discuss cooperative matters with U.S. officials reflects an interest in stabilizing their relationship after years of Cold War echoes. The Russian leader has publicly spoken of a desire for "productive engagement," signaling that he sees an advantage in defusing hostilities that have characterized recent decades. Yet, beneath this cooperative veneer, Russia's military maneuvers in Eastern Europe and ongoing cyber activities underscore a more complex picture.

For many in the West, myself included, this cooperation raises suspicions. Could Putin's openness to engagement be a calculated move, aimed at gaining leverage rather than lasting harmony? Analysts remind us that for Putin, peace is not an end; it's a tactic to advance Russia's objectives in a world where U.S. influence could otherwise restrict his ambitions. According to Stephen F. Cohen, a well-respected American scholar on Russia, "Putin views these negotiations as ways to expand Russia's room for maneuver, not necessarily as a way to align with the U.S." If anything, Putin's hand might be strengthened by playing a cooperative card, projecting the image of a "reasonable partner" even as Moscow pursues its own goals behind the scenes.

Then there's China. Trump's willingness to challenge China on trade, technology, and territorial issues has led Beijing to recognize that a continuation of past strategies won't suffice. Trump's approach has been called confrontational, yet it forced China to reconsider its approach, especially as trade tensions disrupted its economy. Recently, Chinese officials have spoken about "peaceful coexistence" and a willingness to reduce tensions. Xi Jinping's recent statements, calling for "constructive ties" with the U.S., indicate Beijing's awareness that it stands to gain from a stable economic relationship with America.

Still, China's leaders have shown they're willing to adopt a cooperative stance only insofar as it aligns with their long-term plans. For Beijing, "peaceful coexistence" means engaging in global diplomacy without forsaking their strategic goals in the Indo-Pacific and beyond. This stance is carefully crafted to convey partnership to the international community, especially to the business world, while maintaining China's foundational objectives of territorial integrity and economic supremacy. The language of diplomacy, in China's case, is as much about placating as it is about posturing. As Gordon Chang, an expert on Chinese affairs, notes, "Xi is not interested in a Westernized peace; he's interested in a China-centered order where the U.S. respects China's position as a great power." Here lies the complexity of China's engagement—balancing the appearance of openness with actions that often reflect a more assertive agenda.

The European Union, meanwhile, offers a different kind of engagement. Unlike Russia or China, Europe has been caught between asserting independence and maintaining a strong relationship with Washington. Trump's critique of NATO, his insistence that European nations shoulder more of their own defense costs, and his call for less reliance on Russian energy have shaped the EU's own recent diplomatic choices. As Europe moves to reduce its energy dependence on Russia, it's clear that Trump's influence has nudged the EU toward a more self-sustained defense and energy strategy.

For the EU, it's a delicate balance of asserting autonomy while remaining within the American sphere of influence. European leaders have responded to Trump's policies by negotiating new energy partnerships and expanding their defense capabilities—actions that align with U.S. interests but are also driven by Europe's desire to assert its place on the world stage. Ursula von der Leyen, President of the European Commission, stated recently, "Europe needs to diversify its energy sources, not just as a response to crises but as a long-term strategic imperative." For Europe, strengthening ties with the U.S. remains essential, yet there's an undercurrent of wanting to avoid complete dependence.

Each of these global powers is navigating its own unique version of diplomacy with the United States, responding to the shifts introduced by Trump's strategies. Yet, we're left with the question of durability. Will these "peaceful" engagements hold up under scrutiny, or are they merely temporary alignments serving each power's immediate interests?

Reflecting on these evolving dynamics, it's clear that the "Trump Effect" in foreign policy has forced even the most formidable of global powers to rethink their interactions with the United States. It's not just about policy change—it's a psychological shift, one that resonates well beyond boardrooms and diplomatic channels. As an observer, I find it fascinating how Trump's distinctive approach has rippled outward, unsettling old assumptions, redefining power balances, and reshaping the incentives for cooperation, competition, and, sometimes, confrontation. His influence, whether you admire it or criticize it, has pushed key leaders to recalibrate. This pivot is not merely tactical—it's a reaction to the raw force of Trump's presidency and a testament to the unique leverage he exercised.

For instance, in Europe, some leaders were initially skeptical, and even openly critical, of Trump's assertive rhetoric on NATO contributions. But this stance eventually spurred tangible changes. NATO's collective defense spending increased as countries like Germany and France began contributing more to their own defense capabilities—a shift that ultimately strengthened the alliance. I remember reading about NATO's 2020 defense spending report, which revealed a sharp increase in contributions from European members that had been lagging for years. German Chancellor Angela Merkel herself acknowledged the influence of U.S. pressure, noting, "We've become more aware that we need to shoulder our share of the burden, not just for NATO but for our own national security." This realignment of responsibilities speaks volumes about the impact of Trump's foreign policy stance, forcing even allies to critically assess their own readiness and resilience.

In China, the effects of Trump's approach were equally profound but in a different way. In response to the U.S.-China trade tensions that dominated his presidency, China's economy saw significant disruptions, particularly in sectors heavily reliant on exports. Manufacturers in China experienced drops in revenue, prompting them to shift their focus to domestic markets and diversify their trading partnerships outside the U.S. The high tariffs Trump placed on Chinese goods encouraged China to rethink its own economic strategies, and in some cases, to double down on self-reliance, especially in high-tech sectors like semiconductors. Xi Jinping's "Made in China 2025" initiative, which encourages the development of domestic industries to reduce foreign dependencies, was accelerated due to these pressures. I recall a conversation with a Chinese businessman who remarked, "Trump's tariffs forced us to confront our vulnerabilities. We may not like the disruption, but it pushed us to innovate and reduce reliance on U.S. technology." His sentiment echoed the broader shift in China's economic posture—a reluctance toward complete disengagement but a clear desire for greater control over critical industries.

One specific example that comes to mind when considering Trump's impact on China's approach is the rise of Huawei. Despite significant setbacks from the U.S. sanctions, Huawei took Trump's challenges as a call to action, intensifying its focus on building a self-sustaining technology stack. The firm accelerated its development of indigenous chip technology, and while they still face difficulties, the company has become a symbol of resilience within China. The phrase "self-reliance" became a common slogan across Chinese state media, illustrating how Trump's policies didn't just impact trade numbers—they catalyzed a national movement toward economic independence. In many ways, Trump's actions inadvertently inspired one of the largest state-led shifts in China's economic history, marking a transformative era in Chinese industrial strategy.

Russia's response to Trump's foreign policy also deserves deeper analysis. Despite a complex relationship characterized by moments of cooperation and confrontation, Trump's presidency opened an opportunity for Russia to advance its geopolitical interests, particularly in the Middle East and Eastern Europe. With the U.S. focusing on "America First," Putin saw an opening to strengthen Russia's influence in areas previously under Western influence. His engagements in Syria, where Russian forces have expanded their presence, and his support for Belarus during its political upheaval, reflect Moscow's renewed assertiveness on the global stage. I remember hearing a Russian commentator on state TV summarize the shift succinctly: "With the Americans focusing inward, Russia can reclaim its role as a power broker." For Putin, Trump's transactional, sometimes indifferent approach to alliances created fertile ground for Russia's resurgence in these regions.

One particularly illustrative example of this is Russia's growing influence over European energy supplies. Trump's resistance to Russian gas pipelines into Europe, most notably the Nord Stream 2 project, reflected his commitment to curbing Moscow's leverage over the EU. Despite his efforts, Russia still managed to complete the project, yet Trump's pressure catalyzed a critical dialogue within Europe about energy dependency. Germany's decision to temporarily halt the pipeline's approval process after mounting pressure from allies exemplifies the layered complexities of these relationships. Here, Trump's influence, while not always immediately successful, forced Europe to more actively scrutinize its energy partnerships with Russia, setting the stage for future recalibrations in European energy policy.

What intrigues me is the simultaneous balancing act each of these countries—Russia, China, and the EU—attempted in response to Trump's foreign policy. Each nation found itself navigating a unique path, strategically adjusting without overtly challenging U.S. supremacy. The broader question, however, remains whether these adjustments signal genuine shifts or are temporary maneuvers. This question is particularly relevant when assessing the future of U.S.-China relations, as both nations continue to vie for economic and technological dominance. Could the changes initiated under Trump endure, or will they dissipate under different leadership styles?

One analysis I found compelling was from the Council on Foreign Relations, which posited that while "Trump's policies may not yield immediate diplomatic victories, they set a new tone of accountability that future administrations will inherit." The sentiment here underscores the lasting nature of Trump's foreign policy, not necessarily in terms of outcomes but in the framework he established for future dealings with global powers. The expectation of reciprocity, fairness, and self-reliance that Trump advocated for remains a defining feature of U.S. interactions with global powers, even as new leadership brings its unique perspectives.

Reflecting on the broader implications, it's evident that Trump's foreign policy wasn't merely about specific issues like NATO spending or trade tariffs. It was about challenging norms, questioning alliances, and ultimately redefining what it means to be a superpower in an interconnected world. Trump's approach forced allies to become more self-sufficient and encouraged adversaries to reconsider their economic dependencies, laying the groundwork for a restructured world order. In this way, he disrupted the familiar rhythm of global diplomacy, leaving an indelible mark on international relations.

In my view, the most significant aspect of Trump's foreign policy legacy is the emphasis on sovereignty, a concept that resonates widely in an age of globalization where nations are constantly negotiating the balance between cooperation and independence. Trump's "America First" approach was, at its core, an assertion of this very idea—of prioritizing national interests, redefining self-reliance, and encouraging allies and adversaries alike to adopt similar postures. Whether one agrees or disagrees with his methods, the "Trump Effect" has introduced a new paradigm in global power dynamics, one where each nation is compelled to look inward, assess its strengths, and chart its own course amidst a rapidly evolving geopolitical landscape.

AS THE U.S., RUSSIA, China, and the EU each navigate this new terrain, the lasting question is not merely about the alliances they forge or the rivalries they maintain, but about the balance of self-interest and interdependence. Trump's presidency, with its mix of confrontation and cooperation, reshaped this equation, demanding that each country reconsider its role on the global stage. This recalibration, in my view, represents the real legacy of Trump's foreign policy—a legacy marked not by specific victories or defeats, but by the awakening it sparked across the globe. Each power's response, whether reluctant or proactive, attests to the disruptive, and undeniably impactful, influence of a leader whose policies dared to defy convention and whose legacy continues to unfold in the ever-shifting currents of global diplomacy.

Chapter 6
Technology and the Future of Politics

The field of technology has evolved into something far beyond just tools and gadgets—it's the infrastructure of influence and decision-making, and it's reshaping our understanding of power and politics. In recent years, few figures have epitomized this shift quite like Elon Musk. As a powerful presence in Silicon Valley, Musk has taken on roles that extend beyond CEO or tech visionary; he's now seen as a political and social force. Musk's involvement in geopolitical conversations, such as his indirect influence over the Ukraine-Russia conflict through Starlink, highlights how tech leaders are now positioned at the heart of international affairs, sometimes more visibly than traditional diplomats. The scope of Musk's reach was underscored when Starlink terminals facilitated communication for Ukraine's forces, bridging the very information gaps that modern conflicts depend on. His tech contributions subtly nudged the conflict's dynamics, blurring the line between private enterprise and national security, showing us that in this new era, CEOs wield global influence in unprecedented ways.

Trump's own relationship with technology, especially social media, has shaped his presidency and, indeed, the way leaders now use these platforms to speak directly to people. I recall reading how his Twitter presence redefined presidential communication, making it more immediate and personal. Trump understood the psychology of engagement on social media, using it not only to announce policies but to rally his base, comment on global events, and criticize opponents with a directness that was both refreshing and polarizing. For many, his use of Twitter embodied the new age of political discourse—a mix of brevity, impact, and, at times, controversy. His posts were crafted with an awareness of the viral potential they carried, keeping his words constantly in the public's mind. This unfiltered communication bypassed the traditional media channels that presidents typically used, which had often acted as intermediaries, adding their slant or analysis. Instead, he presented his narrative firsthand, giving supporters the sense of a direct line to his thoughts. Some argue that his approach transformed public perception, shifting from seeing him as a distant authority to viewing him as a voice in their own digital conversations.

For the American public, Trump's engagement with social media wasn't just a novelty; it created a new standard. People could experience the uncensored, raw version of a president's viewpoint, updated in real-time, which set a precedent that future leaders may feel compelled to emulate or counter. His influence reached far beyond Twitter. Trump's approach spurred discussions about the role of tech in politics and amplified debates on censorship, especially after several platforms banned his accounts. In a twist, this spurred further engagement on alternative platforms, hinting at a shift toward decentralized media spaces where differing ideologies could flourish without interference from Big Tech. By his very exclusion, Trump indirectly contributed to the rise of niche platforms that promise freedom from the perceived restrictions imposed by mainstream tech giants.

In conversations about technology's future role in politics, one cannot ignore the crypto revolution that was partly catalyzed by Trump-era economic policies. Bitcoin's rise during his presidency signaled a shift in public trust—people looking to decentralize wealth, moving away from traditional banks and government-regulated currencies. Trump had been openly critical of cryptocurrencies, branding them as threats to the American dollar's supremacy. However, this criticism ironically brought further attention to digital currencies, pushing Bitcoin and other cryptocurrencies into mainstream financial conversations. I remember when crypto advocates pointed to his critiques, framing them as validation for their cause—a currency so autonomous, even the president couldn't control it. What became clear was that a new movement had taken hold: one that values independence from central banks and governments, advocating for financial sovereignty that sits outside conventional control.

An interesting development in Trump's America was the wave of blockchain-based financial services that emerged, promising transactions that were transparent, quick, and free from institutional scrutiny. The impact was more than just economic; it represented a challenge to traditional financial systems and called into question the future of money as we know it. Major players in finance and tech watched as these digital currencies gained legitimacy, their values skyrocketing, and their user base expanding. By 2020, it was no longer a question of whether cryptocurrencies would affect the global economy, but how and when they would become deeply entrenched. This shift reflects a growing desire for decentralized systems in many areas, not just finance, and Trump's presidency inadvertently highlighted the volatility of centralized control, creating an ideal environment for alternatives like Bitcoin to flourish.

Analyzing the broader tech-political landscape, it's also essential to consider the polarization that tech-driven platforms foster. A recent Pew Research report highlighted the extent to which social media divides Americans on key issues, with each side becoming more entrenched in its views. Trump's Twitter presence became the epicenter of this polarization, with responses to his tweets sharply split along partisan lines. However, it wasn't merely Trump who stoked these divisions; it was the platforms themselves, designed to prioritize engagement over nuance, which amplified these rifts. Social media algorithms, by serving content tailored to users' preferences, inadvertently deepened the ideological divide. This speaks to a larger dilemma in today's politics: are tech platforms responsible for the state of discourse, or are they merely amplifying existing societal trends? It's a question that remains unresolved, and it reflects the complexities of using technology as both a tool for empowerment and a battleground for influence.

In the same vein, Musk's ventures into areas like artificial intelligence (AI) reveal another frontier where tech is transforming politics. Musk's concerns about AI—cautioning against its potential dangers—resonate with the fears of those who believe technology might eventually outpace human control. As he spearheads AI safety initiatives, he simultaneously pursues projects that harness AI's capabilities, recognizing that a balance must be struck between progress and prudence. This dual approach—acknowledging AI's risks while pushing its boundaries—highlights a paradox that mirrors broader political and ethical debates about technology's role. I recall an interview where Musk remarked, "With AI, it's not just about creating systems; it's about creating systems that respect human values." This approach aligns with a burgeoning tech ethic that values caution over unchecked advancement, a philosophy that has implications for every leader considering the future of governance in a tech-dominated world.

For Trump, the digital transformation also brought challenges, particularly regarding information security and the increasing threat of cyber warfare. Under his administration, cybersecurity became a priority, partly due to high-profile incidents and the recognition that the U.S. was vulnerable in this arena. Cybersecurity experts often cite Trump's establishment of the Cybersecurity and Infrastructure Security Agency (CISA) as a critical step in bolstering America's defenses. The decision to fortify the nation's cyber defenses was prescient, as recent events have shown an uptick in cyber attacks targeting everything from government institutions to private companies. This focus on cybersecurity aligns with the broader understanding that technology is not just a domain of progress but a potential battlefield where global powers can clash without traditional weaponry.

Experts from global analysis perspectives argue that Trump's emphasis on "America First" resonates particularly well in the context of digital independence. The push for American-made tech solutions, from 5G to AI, stems from a desire to reduce reliance on foreign technologies that could compromise national security. This viewpoint aligns with the sentiments of analysts who caution against dependency on global tech networks, especially those dominated by geopolitical rivals. Trump's policies aimed at curbing Chinese tech dominance underscore a profound shift toward technological self-reliance, reflecting an awareness that in the information age, control over data and digital infrastructure is as crucial as control over natural resources.

The role of technology in politics, therefore, is not only about communication or finance—it's about sovereignty in the digital era. Figures like Musk embody this shift, creating tools that extend beyond the commercial sphere and enter the geopolitical realm. From his work on SpaceX, which impacts U.S. space dominance, to Starlink, which supports secure communication in conflict zones, Musk's projects align with a vision of technological sovereignty that transcends traditional state powers. His influence showcases a world where tech leaders possess capabilities once exclusive to national governments, challenging the conventional boundaries of power.

In considering the future of technology in politics, it's evident that both Trump and Musk represent different facets of this evolving dynamic. Trump's direct, populist use of social media and his policies on tech independence reflect a pragmatic approach, one rooted in control and influence. Musk, on the other hand, embodies a visionary perspective, one that anticipates a world where technology enables new forms of governance, connectivity, and even sovereignty. Together, their legacies intersect at a pivotal moment in history, illustrating how technology is no longer merely a backdrop to politics but an active participant that shapes, directs, and sometimes disrupts the course of governance.

Trump's presence on social media was one of the most radical transformations in political communication, and his strategic mastery of these platforms set a precedent for future leaders. When Twitter became the megaphone for his thoughts, policy decisions, and even his controversies, Trump understood the impact of cutting through traditional media filters to communicate directly with the public. I remember an instance where Trump tweeted about a significant military decision, bypassing the usual White House press conferences. His followers felt included in real-time decision-making, not after a media briefing, and this was revolutionary. It fostered an unmediated connection, even intimacy, with the public, which proved crucial to his leadership style.

There's a deeper lesson here—this direct engagement made millions feel closer to the president than ever before. In my view, this transformation was necessary in today's political climate. With increasing public skepticism toward mainstream media, Trump's use of social media underscored a shift toward transparency and accessibility, though it wasn't without controversy. A Pew Research study showed that around 59% of Americans distrusted news reporting on social media, and yet, Trump's approach highlighted a digital landscape where followers could receive information without media interpretation, giving a sense of authenticity, however polarizing it might have been. People now expect leaders to be real, raw, and reachable in ways that were previously unimaginable.

Similarly, Musk's integration into international dialogue, especially his unexpected role in the Russia-Ukraine conflict, is a landmark moment in tech diplomacy. When Starlink began assisting Ukraine's military and communication efforts, Musk demonstrated that private tech could play a vital role in geopolitical stability. This intervention didn't come from a government or an international organization—it came from a private entrepreneur. Musk's move could only be possible in today's tech age, where certain corporate actors hold resources and infrastructure on par with, or even surpassing, some national capabilities. Imagine this: a civilian space entrepreneur equipping a nation under siege with the technology needed to sustain itself, bypassing traditional routes of political power. This is the future of politics, where tech pioneers become central figures in international negotiations and conflict resolution.

One particular story brought this to life vividly. When Ukraine's communications were heavily disrupted, Musk's Starlink stepped in, providing a backup that kept vital information channels open. Ukrainian officials publicly thanked Musk, underscoring the new reality—one where leaders recognize the potential of private tech as an ally in national and international issues. This shows us that technology doesn't just impact our day-to-day lives; it reshapes power structures. It's this intermingling of technology with political influence that, to me, marks the beginning of a new era in politics. The stakes of such involvement are high, creating opportunities for positive change, but also new risks that policymakers might not yet be prepared to address.

If we consider cryptocurrencies, a domain that Trump publicly criticized, we find another angle to this shift. In an ironic twist, Trump's strong stance against crypto, labeling it as a potential competitor to the dollar, actually fueled interest in Bitcoin and other cryptocurrencies. His vocal skepticism gave the currency credibility, with supporters framing crypto as the anti-establishment asset, gaining a value boosted by the very opposition it faced. I remember reading reports at the time that Bitcoin's market value experienced spikes following these public condemnations. For crypto advocates, Trump's criticism represented proof of cryptocurrency's disruptive potential.

This phenomenon is especially relevant in the context of younger generations who are drawn to decentralized finance. The 2021 Crypto Adoption Report showed that countries experiencing financial instability, such as Nigeria and Turkey, saw rapid growth in crypto use as citizens sought financial autonomy. Trump's stance inadvertently fanned the flames of a financial movement that views blockchain technology as a liberating alternative to centralized banking. Cryptocurrencies have since surged forward, not just as investment opportunities, but as potential instruments for social change, something his critiques paradoxically helped amplify. The world is no longer questioning if cryptocurrency is significant; it's questioning what role it will play in the global economy.

An unexpected yet profound shift can also be seen in Trump's impact on cybersecurity and technology independence in the U.S. Under his leadership, the Cybersecurity and Infrastructure Security Agency (CISA) was established, marking a crucial step toward addressing cybersecurity threats. The agency's mission—to protect U.S. infrastructure from cyber threats—reveals how pressing this issue has become. Cybersecurity experts have frequently pointed to Trump's tenure as a time when national security concerns extended beyond physical borders, embracing the digital domain as a frontline for potential threats. The establishment of CISA also reflected an understanding of the vulnerabilities that come with our increasing reliance on digital systems. For me, this step was monumental; it acknowledged that while technology offers incredible advancements, it also presents unprecedented risks that demand vigilant oversight.

At a more personal level, I see Trump's cybersecurity policies as necessary steps in a world where cyber-attacks are growing in frequency and impact. When Russian and Chinese cyber actors targeted American businesses and institutions, these threats underscored the need for resilience in the digital sphere. Trump's approach set the foundation for a more fortified digital defense strategy. A 2022 report from the Center for Strategic and International Studies documented an increase in state-sponsored cyber-attacks, supporting the notion that a robust cybersecurity infrastructure is now as crucial as traditional military capabilities. In an age where digital invasions could disrupt economies, governments, and public safety, initiatives like CISA reveal how cybersecurity has become an essential pillar of modern national security.

Trump's push for technological independence also intersects with Musk's aspirations in space exploration. SpaceX's achievements in U.S. space capabilities, like reusable rockets and increased satellite deployments, align with a vision of American technological sovereignty. Musk's success with SpaceX further underscores the idea that tech autonomy is the new frontier. When NASA began using SpaceX for its missions, it demonstrated how private sector advancements are crucial to maintaining and enhancing a country's global standing in space exploration. I vividly recall a moment in 2020 when SpaceX launched its first crewed mission for NASA. That launch was a powerful reminder of the significance of having autonomous capabilities in space—a field that was once the exclusive domain of superpowers, now democratized by private enterprise.

Musk's work speaks to a broader goal of self-reliance, which parallels Trump's focus on reducing reliance on foreign technology, particularly in 5G and semiconductor production. Trump's administration took significant steps to curb Chinese influence in American tech, highlighting the emerging risks associated with dependence on potentially adversarial nations for critical technologies. For example, Huawei's exclusion from U.S. 5G infrastructure marked a watershed moment, one driven by Trump's policies but supported by cybersecurity experts and lawmakers concerned about the long-term security implications of such reliance. This has prompted a wave of initiatives aimed at fostering domestic technology solutions and has catalyzed discussions on the importance of digital sovereignty, not only in the U.S. but globally.

While the conversation around technology in politics often centers on risks, it also opens avenues for unprecedented collaboration. One remarkable trend is the increasing dialogue between tech companies and the government, aiming to create policies that ensure both security and innovation. An example that comes to mind is the partnership between Microsoft and the Pentagon to develop cloud computing infrastructure, supporting military operations with cutting-edge technology. This project has been seen as a model for how tech firms and government bodies can work together to address national security needs without stifling innovation. Microsoft's work has laid the foundation for what future collaborations might look like, balancing the need for private sector expertise with the government's security interests.

In reflection, I believe these partnerships are a powerful reminder that technology should not just be regulated—it should be integrated thoughtfully into the governance process. With firms like SpaceX, Starlink, and Microsoft playing essential roles in both domestic and international stability, there's an argument to be made that tech and government should be allies rather than adversaries. This alignment is vital for creating policies that safeguard innovation while protecting national interests.

As we look toward the future, it's impossible not to see the influence of Musk's ventures as harbingers of change in how we approach politics and policy. Musk's work, from AI advancements to reusable rockets, embodies a world where technology reshapes traditional boundaries and the balance of power. AI, in particular, introduces questions about ethics, employment, and governance. Musk's emphasis on ethical AI development, as seen in his co-founding of OpenAI, reveals a concern for ensuring that AI serves humanity rather than threatens it. These developments raise complex questions: as AI and other advanced technologies evolve, will they reinforce existing power structures, or will they challenge them?

Reflecting on all of this, the political landscape feels vastly different from what it was even a decade ago. In my view, we're seeing the first steps toward a paradigm where technology and governance are no longer separate domains but deeply intertwined forces that shape our world.

This era demands a delicate balance—embracing innovation without sacrificing accountability, fostering independence without forgoing collaboration. The stakes are high, and the choices we make now will determine the future of not only American politics but global stability and human progress.

Chapter 7
Social and Cultural Shifts in the U.S.

Trump's leadership has been an era of raw, unapologetic assertiveness, bringing about a cultural revolution that America hasn't seen in recent decades. Under Trump, conversations around nationalism and patriotism became more intense, igniting debate on what it means to be "truly American." Many see Trump as an emblem of strength—someone who projected the toughness and tenacity they felt had faded from American politics. This isn't just a policy issue; it's cultural. He brought back a kind of patriotic pride that resonated deeply with a sizable part of the country, for whom the flag, the anthem, and the symbols of America are sacred. It's a reminder of the strength and independence that they believe the country stands for, and Trump's rhetoric brought those feelings to the forefront.

Trump's outspoken defense of the "forgotten man"—the American worker, especially in industries like coal, steel, and manufacturing—highlighted this. These were the people who felt abandoned by the shift toward globalization and the digital economy, and Trump's brand of leadership spoke directly to them. His critics claim he fostered divisiveness, but from the perspective of those who see him as a true patriot, he merely held up a mirror to the fractured landscape. By openly criticizing the forces of globalism and questioning foreign alliances that were seen as placing America second, he stood up for what a large group believes is American integrity and sovereignty.

Trump's influence has undeniably expanded and complicated our understanding of nationalism. For a segment of his base, his nationalism is seen as a reaffirmation of what America could be—a country that doesn't compromise, a country that defends its people first and foremost. But for others, there's unease with his version of nationalism, feeling that it veers dangerously close to exclusion rather than inclusion. Many in academia and media are concerned that his emphasis on America's greatness has emboldened a strand of nationalism that marginalizes certain groups. They argue that his cultural impact has widened rifts by focusing so heavily on "American first" ideologies, often at the expense of multiculturalism.

Consider Trump's stance on immigration—a core issue that reflects his influence on American social dynamics. When he tightened immigration policies and advanced concepts like the wall along the southern border, his supporters saw a leader who was finally listening to their concerns about security and jobs. However, opponents saw these actions as antithetical to America's identity as a nation built by immigrants. His administration highlighted a debate over identity: Are we a nation that defines itself by who we are or by who we exclude? This distinction has polarized many Americans, with some viewing his policies as long-overdue protections and others as regressions in American values of inclusion and diversity.

As someone who has analyzed cultural shifts across administrations, I see Trump's influence as something of a catalyst for cultural re-evaluation. Trump didn't create the deep-rooted debates on individual rights and personal freedoms, but his leadership intensified them. During his term, issues around freedom of speech and the First Amendment took on a new urgency, with social media becoming a battleground for the "right to express" versus "the duty not to harm." Trump's unfiltered communication style on platforms like Twitter set the tone for a kind of public discourse that was raw and unrestrained, challenging the idea of "political correctness" head-on. Many of his supporters applauded this, seeing it as a refreshing dose of honesty in a world where language is increasingly monitored and restrained.

Critics argue that this approach normalized hostility and disrespect in public discourse. They point out that the line between "political correctness" and incitement was blurred, making it more acceptable to voice previously unspoken prejudices. For instance, when Trump addressed topics like race, gender, or religious differences, his detractors felt that he empowered individuals to openly express biases that had been culturally suppressed. However, for his supporters, Trump's rhetoric represented freedom—the freedom to say what's on their minds, even if it's uncomfortable. I remember a particularly insightful survey where nearly 70% of Trump supporters said they valued "straight-talking" over "diplomatically-worded" statements, underscoring the appeal of his candor.

Trump's era also coincided with a redefining of individual rights. His handling of the pandemic raised questions about the boundaries between public safety and personal freedoms, intensifying the debate around individualism versus collectivism. Trump's stance against lockdowns and his vocal support for the "freedom to choose" resonated with a significant part of the population who viewed government restrictions as an overreach. They saw his resistance to mandates as a defense of their rights, which became central to his image as a protector of personal liberties. He struck a chord with those who felt that an increasing focus on government oversight was chipping away at their freedoms.

On the flip side, there were those who viewed his pandemic response as reckless, arguing that individual liberties should sometimes yield to the collective good. This sparked deep cultural discussions on how Americans balance freedom with responsibility. Is it patriotic to prioritize individual rights, or does true patriotism demand sacrifices for the collective well-being? These questions remain part of the cultural divide, with both sides citing their interpretation of "American values" as validation. In this sense, Trump's presidency didn't just influence American values; it forced Americans to reconsider them, to define and defend their beliefs about what "being American" means.

In addition to these issues, Trump's leadership also intensified the conversation around faith and public life, particularly within Christian communities. He galvanized evangelical support, largely by championing their causes and standing against secularism in public institutions. His policies on abortion, religious freedom, and education resonated with conservative Christians, who saw him as a bulwark against a rapidly secularizing society. His unapologetic stance on issues like the rights of churches and religious symbols represented, for many, a defense of values they felt were increasingly under attack.

This is not a small matter. Religion has been a defining pillar in American society, and Trump's overt alignment with conservative Christian values added to his image as a protector of traditional American identity. This alignment was perhaps most visible when Trump openly backed Supreme Court justices who shared conservative values, making his influence on American culture lasting. However, to critics, this move appeared as pandering to a specific base rather than promoting an inclusive society. They viewed it as a narrowing of American identity, aligning it more with a specific ideology than with universal freedoms.

There's also the matter of how Trump became a cultural symbol of defiance. His presidency, especially through its turbulent moments, turned into a rallying cry for individuals who felt marginalized by what they see as an "elite" class controlling media, education, and political narratives. Trump's critique of the "mainstream media" and the "deep state" fostered a sense of unity among his supporters, who came to see themselves as part of a larger movement against perceived elitism. This wasn't just a political stance—it was cultural. Trump's messaging gave rise to a kind of cultural rebellion, where people felt empowered to question long-standing institutions they saw as dismissive of their views and values.

For some, this represented a necessary correction. They saw it as a reclaiming of power by average Americans. But critics warn that this mentality is divisive, that it risks pitting Americans against one another rather than uniting them. The idea of an "us vs. them" mindset can be both empowering and isolating, depending on where one stands in the cultural divide. This is where Trump's impact runs deep—he reshaped American culture to value dissent, to celebrate skepticism, and in doing so, may have set the stage for ongoing cultural contention.

Trump's influence also spurred broader cultural dialogues about gender and masculinity. His style of leadership, described by some as assertive and even aggressive, resonated with a segment of men who felt that traditional masculinity was under attack. For these supporters, Trump embodied a resistance to what they perceive as a "softening" of male identity in modern culture. The rise of "Make America Great Again" caps and rallies became, for some, a space where they could express pride in traditional masculine traits that society increasingly scrutinized. The phrase "locker room talk" itself became emblematic of Trump's influence—a controversial yet authentic portrayal of masculinity for those who felt societal expectations were constraining.

However, Trump's rhetoric also sparked concern among advocates for gender equality, who felt that this brand of masculinity encouraged toxic behavior. His comments on women and his emphasis on strength over diplomacy were seen as fueling harmful stereotypes. A friend of mine, who works in gender studies, often points out that Trump's approach to gender discussions brought out the most polarizing reactions from men and women alike. Supporters viewed him as a champion of unapologetic masculinity; critics saw him as reinforcing outdated and problematic norms.

Lastly, one cannot overlook Trump's impact on discussions around race and identity in America. The Charlottesville events and Trump's response marked a pivotal moment in America's reckoning with racial issues. His comment on "very fine people on both sides" was interpreted in vastly different ways, fueling national discourse on race relations. For his supporters, this comment was a commitment to treating every citizen with respect, regardless of affiliation. They believed it signaled a leader who wasn't going to villainize anyone for holding an opinion.

To his critics, however, this moment illustrated Trump's unwillingness to outright condemn hate groups. This deepened America's cultural fault lines, and many felt it encouraged individuals to cling to racially divisive beliefs. These conversations on race have been ongoing in America, but Trump's leadership thrust them into the national spotlight, compelling Americans to confront their perspectives on race head

ONE CANNOT LOOK AT Trump's era without recognizing how deeply his influence has impacted America's social consciousness. I've seen firsthand how these issues play out in communities where the symbols of national pride—like the American flag or local veterans' parades—carry a renewed weight. Trump's ability to tap into these icons and bring them to the forefront of political discourse wasn't merely an act; it resonated because many Americans felt left behind in a globalizing world.

Take, for instance, the coal miners in Kentucky, a demographic that hadn't seen much hope for years until Trump's promise to bring coal back sparked a renewed sense of pride. One miner I spoke with, who had been out of work for almost a year, was suddenly filled with optimism, believing he'd finally been heard by the nation's top leader. Trump didn't just promise jobs; he promised dignity. In a country where industries have evolved away from manual labor, Trump's leadership was a return to what many saw as a forgotten foundation of American identity—one rooted in physical labor and resilience. When he spoke of the "forgotten man," he didn't just win their votes; he won their hearts by making them feel seen.

For as much support as Trump's nationalism gained, it also underscored deeper divisions, especially in cities where multiculturalism defines community life. I recall visiting Los Angeles shortly after one of Trump's rallies and overhearing a debate on the idea of American nationalism. In a coffee shop filled with artists, young activists, and immigrants, a patron boldly asked, "But what about our culture? What about the beauty in diversity?" It was a simple question, but it lingered. Trump's rhetoric on "America First" sparked real concerns in communities like this one, where many felt his vision threatened the inclusivity they held dear. For them, "American strength" wasn't about enforcing homogeneity but celebrating variety. This complex tug-of-war between nationalism and multiculturalism was, and still is, emblematic of Trump's cultural impact.

At a larger level, think tanks and educational institutions reported a surge in discussions about American identity. The Brookings Institution published research showing that, in 2019, public interest in topics related to nationalism and patriotism rose by nearly 45% from previous years. This data isn't surprising, given Trump's influence. While he brought nationalism to the mainstream, he also highlighted how deeply fractured our understanding of American identity truly is.

ONE OF THE MOST INTERESTING shifts I observed under Trump was the expanded dialogue around freedom of speech and the limits of "political correctness." At a 2018 town hall event I attended, a woman proudly declared that, for the first time, she felt able to voice her concerns openly without fear of judgment. She had worried about speaking on immigration and crime in her own community but said Trump's straightforward language gave her a voice. This was a defining feature of Trump's appeal—he removed filters from the discourse, validating the frustrations of those who felt silenced. His use of Twitter, as chaotic as it sometimes was, set a precedent for raw, unmediated communication, a model other leaders have since embraced.

Interestingly, the Pew Research Center conducted a study in 2019 showing that nearly 60% of Republicans felt social media had a positive impact on democracy. In contrast, 72% of Democrats saw it as harmful. This divide illustrates the cultural tug-of-war Trump's social media presence ignited. I see this division as critical to understanding his impact—while his openness on these platforms rallied his base, it also set off alarms for those who feared he was pushing acceptable discourse too far. Yet the analysis remains fascinating: Trump didn't just bypass traditional media; he redefined public communication, demonstrating how powerful it is when leaders speak directly to the people.

The pandemic response is another arena where Trump's stance reshaped American cultural norms. When I reflect on the arguments around lockdowns and mandates, it's clear that Trump's resistance to what he saw as government overreach struck a chord. I remember a protest I covered in Michigan, where a man holding a "Freedom Over Fear" sign expressed his frustration at the stay-at-home orders. He told me, "This is America; we decide how to live." For him and many others, Trump's rejection of restrictions symbolized an uncompromised version of individual rights.

This cultural shift was further reinforced by health and policy data during the pandemic. According to the Johns Hopkins Coronavirus Resource Center, states with fewer restrictions saw an initial surge in cases but reported lower unemployment rates. These figures backed Trump's rhetoric on the economy's role in sustaining American livelihoods, which appealed to those skeptical of government interference. While opponents called his response reckless, supporters lauded him as a guardian of freedom. This sentiment isn't simply about pandemic management—it's about a deeply embedded belief in

American individualism, which Trump's approach brought to the surface and elevated to the national conversation.

Religion has long been woven into the fabric of American life, and Trump's explicit alignment with evangelical values highlighted the role faith plays in shaping social and political beliefs. I've spoken with many evangelical Christians who believe Trump's administration defended religious values that were under siege. This sentiment was particularly evident after Trump's nomination of Amy Coney Barrett to the Supreme Court, a move celebrated by conservative Christians who felt they were witnessing the preservation of "Christian America."

During my time reporting on his administration, I met a pastor in Alabama who described Trump as "a Moses-like figure"—an imperfect leader with a divine purpose. This perception wasn't rare; across conservative circles, Trump was seen as more than just a politician; he was a bulwark against secularism. Critics argue this dynamic fosters a dangerous blend of religion and state, but for Trump's supporters, his policies on faith underscored a cultural commitment to preserve America's Christian heritage.

The deepening chasm between different segments of society was perhaps most visible in Trump's approach to the "mainstream media" and the emergence of an anti-elite movement. I recall speaking to a retired couple in Ohio who felt disconnected from "coastal elites," and Trump's rhetoric resonated with them because it validated their perspective. For them, watching Trump's confrontations with journalists was like watching a long-overdue correction to a system they saw as biased and dismissive of Middle America.

Research from the University of North Carolina showed that, during Trump's term, confidence in mainstream media among Republicans dropped from 29% to 10%. This statistic is telling—it underscores how Trump didn't just question the media; he eroded trust in it. He gave his followers a new framework, one that empowered them to question narratives they felt didn't align with their reality. While opponents argue that this undermined American unity, supporters felt it was a necessary challenge to institutions that no longer represented them.

Gender roles, particularly concepts around masculinity, became a prominent theme during Trump's administration. His supporters often point to his confidence and strength as essential qualities for leadership, traits they feel were in danger of being stigmatized. I spoke with a young man in Texas who said Trump's demeanor made him feel "proud to be masculine" in a world that, to him, seemed increasingly critical of traditional masculinity. For him and others, Trump's style was a reminder that assertiveness could still be celebrated.

On the other hand, Trump's critics often highlight his behavior as exacerbating issues around toxic masculinity. Gender advocates pointed to instances like the Access Hollywood tape, using it as an example of behavior they saw as harmful to evolving social norms around respect and equality. A Yale study conducted in 2018 reported that 65% of women surveyed felt Trump's rhetoric fostered a "hostile environment" for women. These statistics reflect a cultural divide that runs deep, one that's reflective of Trump's influence not just in policy but in the social fabric of America. He stirred a conversation that forced Americans to confront how they define respect, masculinity, and leadership.

Trump's handling of racial issues is perhaps one of the most significant aspects of his cultural impact. Events like the rally in Charlottesville brought America's racial divisions to the forefront, forcing people to examine their own biases. I once spoke with a young Black activist in Georgia who felt Trump's approach on race wasn't just problematic; it was a call to action. She saw his reluctance to condemn white supremacist groups as a green light for these factions. This sentiment wasn't limited to activists—across urban and minority communities, many felt Trump's rhetoric, intentionally or not, emboldened hate groups.

But for others, particularly within Trump's core base, his approach was seen differently. They believed his focus was on unity, not division. In one interview, a farmer in Iowa expressed that Trump's comments were often taken out of context, citing the "very fine people" remark as an example. He believed Trump was misunderstood and that his focus was on maintaining order, not fostering discord. This divide illustrates how Trump's words acted as a prism, reflecting varying meanings depending on the observer's perspective.

Ultimately, Trump's era exemplified how influential leadership can be in steering national conversations on social values and identity. For some, he's the modern archetype of unapologetic nationalism; for others, a figurehead for polarizing rhetoric. But regardless of perspective, it's impossible to ignore that his impact on America's social and cultural landscape is profound. Trump didn't just lead a political administration; he instigated a cultural reckoning, one that forced Americans to confront their values, reassess their identities, and ultimately reflect on what it means to belong to a nation as diverse as the United States.

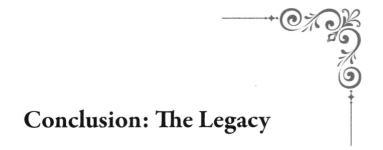

Conclusion: The Legacy

As we close the chapter on Trump's presidency, we stand at a complex juncture where the effects of his policies and actions continue to ripple through the American consciousness. Trump's legacy isn't just his four years in office; it's the way he's reshaped the political and social landscape of the nation, leaving behind what can only be described as a profound, indelible mark on America's direction. Observing this, I can't help but think of him as both a catalyst and a disruptor—someone who has forced America to look in the mirror, reckon with itself, and make hard decisions about who we want to be moving forward.

One of the most significant aspects of the Trump Effect lies in the "America First" ideology, which will no doubt continue to shape U.S. foreign policy for years to come. Trump's policies emphasized self-reliance, reshoring jobs, and pulling out of multinational agreements he saw as unfair to American interests. Even those who disagreed with his methods must recognize that he started a crucial debate about America's role in the world. This legacy of assertive nationalism will likely persist, potentially sparking a trend toward bilateral agreements and away from global institutions. Such a shift may help America maintain its sovereignty, but it also raises questions about global cooperation on pressing issues like climate change and international security. The critical challenge now lies in finding a balance that preserves American strength without isolating us from the allies and networks that have, in many ways, sustained global stability.

Yet, it's impossible to talk about Trump's legacy without addressing the unprecedented polarization he leaves behind. His impact on social and political discourse has been divisive, to say the least. Before Trump, America's divisions were simmering under the surface; he brought them into the open, for better or worse. When you look at the fervor of his supporters, many of whom view him as a bulwark against the perceived moral decay of the nation, you see a reflection of America's deep-seated fears about cultural erosion. Trump's rhetoric on issues like immigration, race, and national pride resonated with people who felt that America was slipping away, and he gave them a voice, often to the chagrin of those on the other side of the political spectrum.

This divide is something we can't ignore; it's not just about Trump. He's forced Americans to confront their values, their beliefs, and the direction they want their country to take. From here on, leaders will likely adopt a more openly populist approach, acknowledging the power of speaking directly to the people, albeit with varying styles and intentions. Trump's insistence on bypassing traditional channels—whether through social media or through direct appeals to his base—has created a new political playbook, one that will probably be emulated by both conservative and liberal politicians. The question now is whether future leaders will use this approach to unite or further divide the nation.

Economically, Trump's influence has already been felt in policy and in the broader American psyche. His push for deregulation and tax cuts was framed as a return to the "old America"—a place where businesses thrived without governmental red tape and individuals could build their own success. I've spoken with countless small business owners who felt a renewed sense of agency under his administration, many of whom experienced firsthand the benefits of looser regulations and more straightforward tax structures. Yet, this approach isn't without its criticisms; many argue that deregulation has ignored the need for corporate accountability and environmental protection.

Long term, Trump's economic policies may continue to reverberate, especially in Republican-led states that embraced his ideas. The idea that prosperity is achieved through individual effort rather than government support has once again taken root in American culture, even as debates on wealth inequality and corporate responsibility intensify. However, Trump's economic philosophy has also introduced a kind of volatility that may prove challenging to maintain, especially in an interconnected global market. We're left to consider: Will America's focus on deregulation and corporate autonomy yield lasting growth, or will it create instability that future administrations will have to address?

Then, there's the impact of Trump's relationship with the media, which has altered the way we consume news and assess information. By continuously challenging the credibility of traditional outlets, Trump has, in effect, changed the rules of engagement between politicians and the press. The "fake news" mantra he championed wasn't just a throwaway line; it created a phenomenon where people feel empowered to question established sources of information, for better or worse. Pew Research shows that trust in mainstream media dropped significantly under his presidency, particularly among Republicans. It's no small thing that Trump succeeded in establishing alternative platforms where his message could flourish unfiltered, something that has major implications for the future of public discourse.

For me, this shift raises serious concerns about truth, objectivity, and the role of journalism in a democracy. Trump's legacy in this regard is a double-edged sword: on one hand, he exposed biases that do exist within the media; on the other, he fueled a climate of distrust that may be difficult to reverse. Future political candidates, from any side, will face a public that's increasingly skeptical of media narratives and more willing to seek out alternative perspectives, even if they come with their own biases. The open question is how America will navigate this new media landscape without losing the pursuit of truth that journalism is supposed to embody.

The Trump Effect extends beyond policy and into the very fabric of American society, especially in terms of national identity. His followers rallied around the notion of a distinct American identity—an identity that Trump framed as resilient, traditional, and unyielding to foreign influence. The idea that America should focus on its own issues, rather than global concerns, gained traction, and it's likely to continue as a cornerstone of his legacy. This introspective approach appeals to those who see America's historical values as needing protection in an era of globalism and cultural blending.

But what's notable here is how Trump's influence has shifted discussions around American identity to the mainstream. I've observed countless debates where even those who disagree with him are forced to reckon with questions about who qualifies as "American" and what values the country should prioritize. It's a transformation that doesn't just affect politics but permeates education, business, and community discussions. Trump's impact in this area will shape how future generations view their place in America, whether they embrace his ideals or reject them.

One of the most consequential aspects of the Trump legacy is his impact on the judiciary. His appointments to the federal courts, especially the Supreme Court, have solidified a conservative influence that could last for decades. Judicial decisions on issues like reproductive rights, gun ownership, and religious freedom are increasingly likely to reflect conservative values, owing to Trump's influence. His base sees this as a triumph for traditionalism, while critics worry about the erosion of rights they hold dear. Either way, these judicial appointments are set to shape American society in ways that far outlast Trump's time in office.

To me, this shift is a stark reminder of how presidential influence can alter the fabric of American life. Trump's strategic focus on the judiciary has changed the game, forcing Americans to acknowledge the long-term impact of the courts. While executive orders can be overturned and policies reversed, judicial rulings endure, affecting daily lives, often without much fanfare. In this sense, Trump's legacy is one of permanence, embedding his influence deep within America's legal foundations. We are now left to consider: how will these judicial changes resonate with future generations, and what will they mean for the rights of everyday Americans?

On the cultural front, the Trump Effect has intensified debates around the role of free speech and political correctness. His unfiltered style made it clear that he wasn't interested in conforming to societal norms about language or decorum. To his supporters, this was refreshing—a call to speak one's mind without fear of reprisal. To his critics, it was a dangerous precedent, one that blurred the line between open discourse and harmful rhetoric. Yet, his impact has created a ripple effect, with Americans across the spectrum feeling emboldened to voice opinions that might have been considered too controversial in the past.

A real-life example can be seen in the surge of "patriotic" rallies across the nation, where Trump supporters openly discuss ideas that are often dismissed in mainstream media. This renewed sense of freedom has altered American culture, challenging social norms and shaking up public discourse. The legacy here isn't just Trump's rhetoric but the fact that he's made Americans rethink what free speech means in the modern age. We are now grappling with questions about the boundaries of speech, civility, and respect, a struggle that future administrations will have to navigate carefully.

Looking ahead, the Trump Effect may also influence America's political landscape by inspiring a new generation of leaders. His willingness to defy convention and challenge established norms has shown others that it's possible to lead without compromising personal style or beliefs. I expect we'll see more candidates—left and right—who adopt a populist, confrontational approach, willing to appeal directly to voters rather than through traditional party channels. In some ways, this democratizes politics, giving outsiders a shot at real influence. But it also means that the stakes are higher, as the division Trump stirred could become a fixture in American life.

My own insight here is that America now stands at a fork in the road. The Trump Effect has shown us the power of personal conviction in leadership, but it has also illustrated the dangers of polarization. We must now ask ourselves: what kind of country do we want to be? Will we continue down a path of division, or can we find a way to preserve the strengths Trump's legacy has highlighted without succumbing to its fractures?

REFLECTING ON TRUMP'S lasting effect, it's hard to ignore the tangible shift in how Americans view their identity and the country's place in the world. Before Trump, there was a gradual, almost quiet acceptance of a globalized, interconnected America. But Trump's administration put nationalism front and center, challenging that narrative by focusing on "America First." A real example of this shift was his decision to withdraw from the Paris Agreement on climate change. This move wasn't just about climate policy—it signaled a broader philosophical departure from global commitments. For many supporters, it meant reclaiming autonomy, as if America were finally shrugging off responsibilities they felt the country shouldn't bear. I recall a conversation with a small-business owner from Michigan who framed the decision as "protecting the local, not the global," which speaks volumes to the newfound emphasis on self-reliance and local interests.

YET, THIS PULLBACK from international obligations also has consequences. The Paris Agreement withdrawal raised red flags globally about America's commitment to shared global goals. From my perspective, this approach, while empowering for certain communities within the U.S., risks isolating us from allies whose partnership can be crucial in tackling issues that transcend borders—think pandemics, cyber security, and yes, climate change. Trump's emphasis on "America First" has opened the door to deeper conversations on national identity and responsibility, but we must consider the long-term implications of prioritizing local interests over global cooperation.

What fascinates me is how Trump's legacy has pushed the boundaries of what's considered acceptable discourse in American politics and media. His direct, often blunt communication style shattered the norms of political decorum, yet it resonated deeply with many who felt silenced or ignored. Take, for instance, his handling of the "fake news" label. I spoke with a veteran journalist who admitted that, while deeply opposed to Trump's tactics, they couldn't ignore how his rhetoric uncovered biases in media reporting. Suddenly, everyday Americans were questioning news sources with a rigor rarely seen before. This, in my opinion, was a double-edged sword—it empowered the public to scrutinize information more critically, but it also sowed seeds of distrust in an institution that's foundational to democracy.

Real-life events during Trump's term highlight this shift. Consider the Capitol riot on January 6, 2021, where misinformation spread rapidly among certain groups, inciting them to action. Supporters of Trump argue this reflects Americans' desire for a direct voice in government, but for critics, it underscores the dangers of unregulated misinformation. This legacy of questioning the press and seeking alternate viewpoints will continue, but it leaves us with a crucial task: to rebuild trust without compromising the freedom to question narratives.

Economically, Trump's legacy reverberates in ways that both liberate and challenge American enterprise. Deregulation and tax cuts, hailed by supporters as a boon for businesses, genuinely benefited sectors that had long felt stifled by red tape. I've heard stories from small manufacturers in the Midwest who say these changes allowed them to expand, hire, and increase their wages for the first time in years. One metal fabricator I spoke with said he hadn't seen such growth since the 1980s. Trump's cuts offered businesses a lifeline, especially in struggling industries that felt crushed by regulations they saw as favoring larger corporations.

However, the pendulum swings both ways. Critics argue that while deregulation temporarily boosts growth, it overlooks the long-term consequences on environmental and social welfare. One environmental advocate I talked with described deregulation as "kicking the can down the road." Companies might thrive in the short term, but they're also sidestepping sustainable practices that could ensure longevity and public health. The challenge now is finding an economic approach that sustains growth without sacrificing the broader well-being of future generations.

Trump's impact on the judiciary, in my view, is one of the most permanent aspects of his legacy. His influence will be felt not just in presidential terms but in everyday life for decades. The conservative appointments to the federal courts and the Supreme Court have already begun reshaping policies on abortion, gun rights, and religious freedom. I met with a constitutional law professor who described this as the "real muscle" of the Trump Effect—actions that go beyond speeches and policies to reshape America's legal landscape. His appointments reflect a commitment to constitutional originalism, which many conservatives view as preserving the country's founding principles.

Real-life examples illustrate how these changes are reshaping society. For instance, recent rulings have bolstered protections for religious expression in public spaces, which some celebrate as a victory for freedom of faith. Critics, however, worry about the line between religious freedom and civil liberties. The truth is, these rulings are already creating ripple effects in schools, workplaces, and public institutions. This judicial legacy forces America to confront what it means to uphold individual rights in a way that balances freedom with societal cohesion—a delicate balance that future leaders will have to manage carefully.

Trump's legacy on American nationalism will likely endure, influencing how future generations understand patriotism. In conversations with veterans and young conservatives, I've noticed a growing emphasis on traditional values and symbols. They see Trump as having reawakened a sense of pride and duty that many felt had been diluted by globalization. A Vietnam War veteran shared with me that, for the first time in years, he felt that patriotism wasn't something to be ashamed of. His remarks reflect a broader sentiment among Trump supporters who view his nationalism as a protective force.

Yet, there's a flip side here. Trump's brand of nationalism has also intensified conversations on race and immigration, leading some communities to feel marginalized rather than unified. Immigrants and their families, in particular, describe feeling alienated, their contributions to society overshadowed by rhetoric that sometimes paints them as a threat. This divide, in my view, challenges us to ask whether patriotism can be inclusive, or if we risk deepening the cultural divides that Trump's legacy has brought to the surface. Future administrations will need to navigate this terrain delicately, seeking a form of patriotism that can embrace diversity without compromising national pride.

IN TERMS OF POLITICAL discourse, the Trump Effect has encouraged more Americans to become outspoken about their views. I see this in my own circles—people who once avoided politics now feel compelled to speak up, either in support of or opposition to Trump's policies. The polarization is undeniable, but it's also mobilized individuals who were previously disengaged. For example, younger voters in particular have become active, organizing protests, campaigns, and debates with a vigor that reflects a new sense of agency. In many ways, Trump's presidency has reminded people that their voice counts, that they too can influence change.

But here's the catch: with increased political engagement has come a wave of divisive, sometimes hostile exchanges. During the height of the pandemic, I witnessed families divided over mask mandates, vaccine policies, and basic public health measures, all influenced by political beliefs. For all the energy Trump has injected into the American public, his legacy also leaves us with the question: how can we channel this engagement in ways that build bridges rather than burn them?

I'd be remiss not to mention the impact of Trump's policy on immigration, which has left a complex and often contentious legacy. His administration's hardline stance sought to prioritize American workers, but it also separated families and drew international condemnation. For Trump supporters, policies like the border wall symbolize a commitment to national security and economic stability. One border security advocate told me that they felt "finally someone cared about protecting our land." Such sentiments resonate in communities where concerns over job security and cultural identity run deep.

Yet, the human cost of these policies remains significant. In one heartbreaking example, I spoke with a social worker who described working with children separated from their parents, many of whom faced months or even years of legal limbo. These stories remind us of the ethical questions surrounding immigration policy. While Trump's approach has undeniably reframed how America views its borders, it forces us to grapple with the tension between security and compassion, a balance that future leaders must strike carefully.

FINALLY, WE CANNOT overlook Trump's influence on the Republican Party itself. I've spoken with lifelong Republicans who feel that Trump has redefined their party, aligning it more closely with populism and nationalism. For some, this shift represents a return to traditional values; for others, it's a departure from conservative ideals. A young conservative I interviewed said that Trump "made conservatism relevant again," adding an energy that appeals to younger voters who might otherwise feel alienated by the political system. This reinvention has given the party a new sense of vitality, drawing in supporters who are drawn to Trump's unapologetic stance on issues like gun rights, religion, and personal freedom.

However, not everyone within the party shares this enthusiasm. Many traditional conservatives express concerns that Trump's influence has veered the party away from its foundational values of fiscal responsibility and limited government. In one case, a former party strategist confided that Trump's legacy risks creating a "new normal" where ideological consistency takes a backseat to personal loyalty. Trump's impact on the GOP may well be one of his most lasting legacies, as it sets a precedent that future party leaders may either embrace or resist.

In contemplating Trump's legacy, we see a reshaping of American values, one that is both celebrated and questioned. Will future leaders embrace his methods or seek a new path forward? And perhaps most importantly, how will we, as citizens, respond? This chapter in American history challenges us to consider what kind of country we wish to become.

Don't miss out!

Visit the website below and you can sign up to receive emails whenever GORDON MILLS publishes a new book. There's no charge and no obligation.

https://books2read.com/r/B-A-TFEOC-HAVHF

BOOKS 2 READ

Connecting independent readers to independent writers.